WOMAN

Created to Help

Titilayo Akinniyi

WOMAN – Created to Help

Acknowledgement

I give all glory and honour to God, the Giver of Good and Perfect Gifts. Thank You Lord for divine inspiration.

My ever-caring husband and helper of my destiny, Engineer Olusegun Akinniyi.

Your patience editing the book and making it ready for publishing is much appreciated.

My Princesses, Oluwakemi and Olayinka Akinniyi. The Prince in the house, Olusegun Oluwatobiloba Akinniyi.

I deeply appreciate Olayinka Akinniyi for her effort in designing the book cover. You did a great job.

Oluwakemi my ever ready and on time flyer designer, what a great gift you are to me.

WOMAN – Created to Help

Oluwatobiloba, the Creativity Manager. Your attention to details made the editing of the book so seamless.

You all made my life so easy and beautiful.

I greatly appreciate you all for your support.

God bless and honour you all.

WOMAN – Created to Help

Dedication

This book is dedicated to GOD and to every WOMAN created by

GOD for His divine purpose on earth.

You are a precious gift from God to Humanity.

WOMAN – Created to Help

Table of Contents

Contents

WOMAN – Created to Help

CHAPTER 1 - WOMAN OR HELPER?

Sometimes, a woman does not know exactly who she is. We live in a complex world where societies define a woman in terms of roles that have been prescribed for her.

I believe as a female child, the expectation of all is that she was born to bear some burdens. A girl who would grow up to become a good woman and wife is expected to function well at home and be exceptional at domestic runs, get the laundry done, done well and on time. If the house is untidy, the first point of call is the female child. She is also the one that has to cook for her brothers even when they are old enough to cook for themselves and others. Which means she must be a good cook, otherwise references would be made to remind her of her marital future. She is expected to eat like a woman and sit with her legs closed while the male can sit as it pleases him. She is also the designated nanny and is

WOMAN – Created to Help

expected to play the mother role to the younger ones when their mother is not available.

The girl realises as she grows up that her male cousins and siblings don't have to observe the same strict set of rules that society has prescribed for her. Then she recoils and starts to ask questions, "Why am I the only one washing the plates, doing all the cooking, mopping the floor and cleaning the windows?" And then she gets told that when she grows up and gets married, she will be better prepared to do all the chores and cooking for her husband. But not all male children are being trained to be good cooks. Why? Simply because they will be married to a woman.

You would think that when she becomes an adult, she would be free from all these responsibilities – both reasonable and unreasonable, right? Far from it! Womanhood comes with another round of responsibilities.

Are we saying that we are created to shoulder someone else's responsibilities as women? Kind of. Why? This is because we were created to help.

WOMAN – Created to Help

Our main assignment from God is to be helpers to the men. That does not make us inferior to them but puts us at the advantage of being the most sought after. Nor does it make them more privileged beings. Without the woman, I would say the world is not really complete. God created them male and female.

Parents, especially women, when you go to that labour room and the midwives tell you that you have just given birth to a baby girl, you should be full of joy because you have just made a great mark on the earth by bringing forth another helper of humanity. What a privilege!

Even every man should be glad to have a female child who will in future be there to take care of him in his old age. A female child is a special gift from God to every family and to the world at large.

The Question of Identity

Understanding one's identity is a crucial first step to take in living a fulfilled life.

WOMAN – Created to Help

Man has always been in search of who he is, why he was created and the purpose for which he was created. When I say man, I am referring to both male and female. The lack of the knowledge of our purpose in life only results in frustration and a dead end. If we do not know the purpose of our existence, we live a life that is full of agitations, hopelessness and the most expensive part of it – living another man's life or vision. No one is created a photocopy of another person. You are always an original in God's image. No man created by God is without a particular destiny, vision, or a definite assignment. As we all know, God is not a waster of resources. He will never create a thing for creating sake without having any use for that thing.

We need to know that every man or woman is on an assignment. That assignment is your purpose in life. To live a fulfilled life, everyone must find out what that purpose or assignment in life is. Sometimes we are so confused about what we are here for or what exactly our purpose in life is. We get so restless not knowing which direction to go.

WOMAN – Created to Help

The Bible says in Hosea 4:6

"My people are destroyed for lack of knowledge"

Notice, it is that *my* people perish for lack of knowledge. This verse is talking about God's people perishing, getting frustrated and not knowing why they have been created.

Remember that God has not created any man or woman accidentally or without a purpose.

Someone says, there may be accidental parents, but there is no accidental baby. Everyone was created by God for a divine purpose. And this is to bring glory and honour to His name.

God does not waste resources. Jesus asked his disciples to gather the crumbs left after feeding the 5000 people. You may wonder why breadcrumbs were so important that they could not be left for the birds of the air to eat.

If breadcrumbs and fish remnant were that important to Jesus, then, your life must be of greater importance to God.

Matthew 15:20

WOMAN – Created to Help

20 And they did all eat, and were filled: and they took up of the fragments that remained twelve baskets full.

Never look down on yourself as a nobody. It cost God His only begotten son to reconcile you and me back to Himself.

We cannot fully understand the depth of His love for us. Who are we that God is so mindful of us?

Psalm 8:4-6

4 What is man, that thou art mindful of him? and the son of man, that thou visitest him?

5 For thou hast made him a little lower than the angels, and hast crowned him with glory and honour.

6 Thou madest him to have dominion over the works of thy hands; thou hast put all things under his feet:

Tell yourself with confidence in God, "I am very important in God's plan for the good of the world".

Definition of Identity

Let's get a clear definition of 'identity':

WOMAN – Created to Help

- Identity is a condition of being yourself and not another person

- It means your personality, your uniqueness, who you really are that no other person is

- Your character which defines who you really are

- What you are made for

From these definitions, we can see that no two people are exactly alike when it comes to identity. Even identical twins are different. To outsiders, they may look alike but their mother knows who is who. Their finger prints are different. Even their voices may sound the same, the pitch in human voice is different creating different sound.

There is no one who is exactly like you in the entire world. You are an original and you must stop trying to be who God has not created you to be. Never try to be the photocopy of anyone. You are an original.

WOMAN – Created to Help

Sometimes we want to be like Mrs. X without knowing what she is going through or has gone through. If you know what Mrs. X is going through or the load she is carrying, you will fast and pray never to be anything close to her.

Be confident about yourself. No one is better than you.

Proverbs 23:7 says

As he thinks in his heart so is he.

CHAPTER 2 - A WOMAN'S IDENTITY

You Are Created with an Identity

Different societies place different values on a woman, and this could create confusion for the average woman. It gets even more confusing when a woman intermarries from one culture into another.

In one culture, the bride's family is expected to pay dowry to the groom's family but in another culture, it is the exact opposite.

In some cultures, the woman is meant to be at the back, to be seen and not to be heard. In other cultures, everybody, including the woman, has a right to be heard.

A woman is defined differently by different societies and cultures and we are left wondering where to turn to for a clear definition of our identity.

Every woman must be able to find answers to such questions as:

- Who am I?

WOMAN – Created to Help

- What is my purpose in life as a woman?

- And if you are married, what is my role in the life of my husband?

Who is a Woman?

Now that we know what identity stands for, who is a woman? A woman is defined as a female human being. The word woman is usually reserved for an adult. Many women define themselves according to their physical appearance or what they do or have. But let us see where the word woman was first mentioned in the Bible.

With all the power and comfort that Adam enjoyed in the garden of Eden, he lacked something very important. There was a vacuum in Adam's life which God was quick to acknowledge because He is such a caring Father.

Woman, you are a vacuum filler. All the animals and plants in the garden of Eden could not fill the vacuum in Adam's life. Then God

WOMAN – Created to Help

gave him someone like himself. Created in God's image. And Adam named the gift as woman.

Genesis 2:23 tells us that the moment Adam saw this gift, he knew exactly where she came from and what she was made from. He said the bone of my bone and flesh of my flesh, she shall be called a WOMAN.

Genesis 2:23

23 And Adam said, This is now bone of my bones, and flesh of my flesh: she shall be called Woman, because she was taken out of Man.

The Bible tells us that God caused a deep sleep to fall upon Adam before taking a rib out of him to create Eve. The moment Adam set his eyes on Eve, he knew she came from him. So how did he know that Eve came from him? The only plausible thing I can think of is that he was asleep physically but not spiritually. He was spiritually alert. Men are the prophets of their homes. A sleeping prophet may completely miss the plan of God for his family and unfortunately, his wife may not be able to help him. The man is the recipient of

WOMAN – Created to Help

God's masterplan; God gives him a wife to help him get to his destination. Do not be passive in your home or marriage as the head of the family. This could be very dangerous for the next generation (your children), your wife and even you. Be a man of purpose and lead your family as God would like you to.

God gave Adam a gift and Adam named the gift. What name did your husband give you? Did he see you as a good gift from God or something that he acquired like a piece of furniture to show that he is a man?

How much value can you add to your husband's life and destiny to make him give you a good name? Your input to your husband's destiny says a lot about the fulfilment of your God-given assignment in his life.

If you are single or divorced, there are always some people God created you for to help in realising their God given assignments. Being single or divorced does not make you a lesser woman or a woman without a divine purpose.

WOMAN – Created to Help

How Does God Define Women?

Genesis 2:18

18 And the Lord God said, "It is not good that man should be alone; I will make him a helper comparable to him."

Which means, in the mind of God, a woman is a helper, a counterpart and a companion.

Who is a Helper?

thefreedictionary.com defines Helper as a person who contributes to the fulfillment of a need or furtherance of an effort or purpose. It means someone who makes it easier for another person to do something.

Genesis 2:18

18 And the Lord God said, It is not good that the man should be alone; I will make him an help meet for him.

God saw something in Adam that was not going on well. Adam was not fulfilling God's plan so God had to come to his rescue.

WOMAN – Created to Help

God said it was not good for a man to be alone. I would put it in another way and say, it not good for a man to live below his God-given potentials. Adam was not fully showcasing the blessings of God in his life. He was at the level of chasing a thousand; way below what he should be achieving.

God, a loving father, decided to help His son Adam and gave him a gift that would make his journey in life pleasurable, fulfilling and fruitful. Adam received from God a Helper that was comparable to him.

The woman as a helper is a gift from God to humanity.

A Helper is a gift from God. Every woman is a divine gift from God to a man. You cannot receive anything except you have been given from above. A woman is very special to the Almighty God. When God gives a gift to anyone, it is for the good and benefit of that person. Every woman is a good and perfect gift to the man chosen by God.

WOMAN – Created to Help

That is why every single lady must hope and trust in God to be given to the man that God has chosen for her. Do not be in a hurry to give yourself to a man.

May I say here that no parent should take God's place in the lives of their children. What I am saying is that, parents must not force their children to be married to someone that they THINK is suitable for them. Instead, they should partner with God with humble heart to turn their children to good and perfect gifts. Jesus said, "Follow Me and I will make you…." The making is by God not by man. Which means, no man can make his own helper. No parent, outside God's plan, can make their daughter a helper to a man. Also, no woman can make herself a successful helper to any man without God's help.

Why should we put ourselves in the place of God? Allow your child to follow God who makes and builds.

God makes and He gives.

Proverbs 23:4

Do not overwork to be rich;

WOMAN – Created to Help

Because of your own understanding, cease!

CHAPTER 3 - BEING A HELPER

Attributes of a Helper

1) She is Godly

She sees other people as God sees them. She does not belittle anybody. She fears God. Her beauty is not only in things that do perish but in heavenly things as she serves humanity for the sake of the kingdom of God. The things of God are the most important in her life. She follows God's instructions to be a good wife to her husband and a helper to many.

Proverbs 31:30

30 Favour is deceitful, and beauty is vain: but a woman that feareth the Lord, she shall be praised.

2) She is loving

Love is one of the characters of God. It is the Name of God. Because she was made by God, she exhibits the character of God. She loves unconditionally, no matter who you are or what you do.

WOMAN – Created to Help

Her love for her husband surpasses feelings. She loves her husband the way God commands every married woman.

Ephesians 5:21-24

21 Submitting yourselves one to another in the fear of God.

22 Wives, submit yourselves unto your own husbands, as unto the Lord.

23 For the husband is the head of the wife, even as Christ is the head of the church: and he is the saviour of the body.

24 Therefore as the church is subject unto Christ, so let the wives be to their own husbands in every thing.

She shows genuine love to her in-laws and people around her.

3) She is full of strength

She can withstand the pressure that comes with the responsibility of being a helper. Being a helper means you must provide the necessary assistance that is required from you. That is, the helper must be strong enough to help. Remember you cannot give what

WOMAN – Created to Help

you do not have. She makes God the source of her strength by feeding daily on the word of God and seeking divine strength. Her gaze is continually on God.

Psalm 5:3

3 My voice shalt thou hear in the morning, O Lord; in the morning will I direct my prayer unto thee, and will look up.

Psalm 121:1-3

1 I will lift up mine eyes unto the hills, from whence cometh my help.

2 My help cometh from the Lord, which made heaven and earth.

3 He will not suffer thy foot to be moved: he that keepeth thee will not slumber.

4) She is available

She is always available for her husband anytime she is needed. No excuses.

WOMAN – Created to Help

Availability as a wife does not end on the bed to satisfy your husband sexually. You must be available to help him emotionally. You must be the first person he sees when he is going through rough times.

Words of encouragement from a wife to her husband may be all that he needs to come out of the ugly situation that he is in. These words are like sweet melody in the heart of the husband. Allow him to lean on your spiritual shoulders. They are meant for him in his time of emotional need.

5) She is not easily upset

She does not allow negative words from people (in-laws or friends) to upset or distract her from her purpose as a helper to her husband. The Bible says that the voice of God is powerful. She allows herself to hear the voice of God, not the negative voices of the enemies in her marriage. There is a way the Almighty God sets you free from being bothered about the damaging comments that people make about you. You will not be bothered at all, instead

WOMAN – Created to Help

you will keep rejoicing and they will be wondering if you are a normal woman. Just tell them it is the grace of God in your life.

6) She is not vengeful

She believes that people act according to their level of understanding or maturity and have the tendency to behave better when they know better. So, she does not see the need to avenge herself of any negative behaviour from anyone. She is not bent on revenge. She leaves it to God to act on her behalf.

Romans 12:19

19 Dearly beloved, avenge not yourselves, but rather give place unto wrath: for it is written, Vengeance is mine; I will repay, saith the Lord.

7) She is full of compassion

She feels what her husband feels whenever he is going through challenges.   She does not isolate herself from the situation faced by the husband. For her, marriage is not a case of "for better I stay

WOMAN – Created to Help

and for worse I run". My counsel to every married woman is that, it is better to stay. You never can tell what tomorrow holds for your husband. In every man is a seed of greatness.

If you are a woman who places so much value on material possessions, you will not be able to cope with the difficult time when your husband needs you most. There is always a low point in everyone's life. A true woman or helper stays on to fight for her husband in the place of prayer.

She believes in the power of a praying wife. She takes her place to seek solution from God on her knees knowing that battles are real and can be won in the realm of the spirit.

2 Corinthians 10:3-5

3 For though we walk in the flesh, we do not war after the flesh:

4 (For the weapons of our warfare are not carnal, but mighty through God to the pulling down of strong holds;)

5 Casting down imaginations, and every high thing that exalteth itself against the knowledge of God, and bringing into captivity every thought to the obedience of Christ;

WOMAN – Created to Help

How to Be an Effective Helper

We are effective when we successfully produce a desired or intended result. You can only be effective in doing something if you understand what you are trying to do, why you are doing it, how to do it, when you need to do it, where to do it and who should do it.

Knowledge is a key factor in becoming an effective helper. The following tips will be helpful on your way to becoming an effective helper.

1) Know Who God Is

The knowledge of God is key to success in a man's life. If you know Him, your journey in life will be with clarity and speed. If you do not know your Creator who made you for a purpose, how are you going to know what purpose to fulfil? Every other person's objective will look like yours and you will be

WOMAN – Created to Help

pursuing the wrong goal all your life. Knowing God puts you on the right path in life.

The word of God in Psalms 16:11 tells us about the benefit of being in the presence of God.

Psalms 16:11

Thou wilt shew me the path of life: in thy presence is fulness of joy; at thy right hand there are pleasures for evermore.

Daniel 11:32b

32b but the people who know their God shall be strong, and carry out great exploits.

Until we know Him, we cannot find the path of life or do great exploits.

2) Know Your Purpose on Earth

WOMAN – Created to Help

Purpose is the reason why a thing was made. Everything of value is made for a purpose. As a woman, you must know why you were created and if your strength is enough for your assignment or not. If your strength is not enough for your assignment, how are you going to help?

In a country with temperatures of 50 degree Celsius, you don't give someone a winter coat that is made to withstand a temperature of -70 degree Celsius. Instead of blessing you for the gift, the receiver may curse you. It does not make any sense at all. God created you because you made sense in his mind. Blessings are products of relevance or fulfilled purpose. If a woman is not relevant in the life of her husband, his life may end up in deficit instead of surplus. NO VAT (Value Added Tax).

Knowing your purpose will make life sweet and enjoyable. It makes your path to destiny smooth and your arrival to your destination quicker or faster. When you don't know your purpose, getting to your destination becomes rough and frustrating. Even your husband that you are supposed to help will be frustrated. Every place looks like your destination and every man looks like your God-ordained husband.

Note that it is not every dress at the fashion store that is your size and not every dress is made for you. God made yours with your name tag on it. There is a God-ordained man or husband with your name tag on him. There is that MR. for whom you are the right MRS.

Ecclesiastes 10:15

15 The labour of the foolish wearieth every one of them, because he knoweth not how to go to the city.

3) Run your purpose

Joel 2:8

8 Neither shall one thrust another; they shall walk every one in his path: and when they fall upon the sword, they shall not be wounded.

WOMAN – Created to Help

In the race of life, there is a specific assignment for each person and each person is assigned a specific lane to run his race. There is more than enough space for all to run the race of life. I do not have to run yours and you do not have to run mine. Neither do I have to wait for you or run with you. My assignment is tagged with the time allotted to it by God.

The scripture says neither shall one thrust another. When you know what you are running for, where you are running to and why you are running, no one will be able to distract you as a woman from running the race that has been set before you in that man's life.

It is not just knowing a purpose that matters, what matters is knowing and putting it to work. You may know a thing, have it and then decide to put it in storage to gather dust. When you know who you are and what you are to do on earth with the precious time God has given you, you need to run with it.

WOMAN – Created to Help

It is very important to run with your purpose. Any woman who refuses to run with her purpose will soon be overtaken by a strange woman. That shall not be your lot in Jesus name.

4) Equip Yourself for Your Purpose

Knowledge they say is power. Knowledge is light. It makes walking or running easy. The Bible says that my people are destroyed for lack of knowledge. Ignorance is a destroyer of destiny.

Get the necessary training for your purpose. I believe that the First Ladies of great countries like the United Kingdom and America receive special training the moment their husbands become Prime Minister or President. Anyone who marries into

WOMAN – Created to Help

the royal family must be well equipped for their royal assignments within the family – how to greet the Queen, how to eat, what to wear and how to speak in public.

How many women take the time to acquire knowledge about what it takes to be a good helpmeet for their husbands? Most women are looking for good houses, cars and dresses. We think being a great wife takes little or no effort. A woman who has the intention of becoming a great helper must be determined to work it out, taking in every word of God about how to be an effective helper or home builder. Godly wisdom is of high importance in your journey as a helper.

James1:5

5 If any of you lack wisdom, let him ask of God, that giveth to all men liberally, and upbraideth not; and it shall be given him.

A woman who is created to be a pastor's wife should equip herself with what it takes to be a helpmeet for the man of God.

WOMAN – Created to Help

You cannot be too reserved as a Pastor's wife to talk to church members. You need to ask for grace in that area. You must be prayerful and hospitable. You must be able to tolerate church members calling your husband throughout the day. It is part of the assignment. You were created for that man to make life easier for him in pursuing his God-given assignment.

The wife of a medical doctor must have some knowledge of what her husband does. A footballer's wife must know about game tactics, her husband's colleagues, the colour and number of her husband's jersey, and the name of his club. Every woman must be able to communicate intelligently in the presence of her husband's friends.

Whatever God has called your husband to do is a pointer to what you must be knowledgeable about. Be relevant in his life.

WOMAN – Created to Help

5) Provide the necessary support

Now that you have acquired the necessary knowledge, use it for the benefit of your man. Do not hold back. Not even your money. Sometimes your husband may need some money and you have it. Be ready to help him. Free yourself from the evils that money brings into homes. Do not get into unhealthy financial competition with your husband. He has $5million, so you must have $10million. Don't waste the time you should invest in your husband pursuing vain things. Stop combining morning, afternoon and evening shifts for the sake of money. If your job requires you to travel a lot, discuss with your husband for approval and make sure he has all the details of your itinerary. If there is a change in your schedule, let him know. Communicate in detail. Erase any form of suspicion.

1 Timothy 6:10

10 For the love of money is the root of all evil: which while some coveted after, they have erred from the faith, and pierced

WOMAN – Created to Help

themselves through with many sorrows.

1 Timothy 6:10

10 For the love of money is the root of all evil: which while some coveted after, they have erred from the faith, and pierced themselves through with many sorrows.

Never love money more than your family. You were created because of them. A Godly woman will always attract favour and honour.

For some women, sex time is snoring time. That is the time some women want to apply liniment or ointment to their joints because they have over-worked themselves doing overtime at work. Remember that money has wings and can fly. What will remain is how relevant you are to your husband and children.

Just because a woman should be financially free does not mean that you should spend the quality time meant for your husband to run after money. There are so many businesses that

WOMAN – Created to Help

can be done from home. Start a day home, a cooking business or other home-based businesses like baking or craft making. Many online businesses can be done from the comfort of your home. Get the necessary training if need be. Look for the business that is suitable for you and stay close to your family.

A home that is void of parental presence cannot be a secure home for the children.

6) Pray for your husband always

Your success as a woman is tied to that of your husband. His success is your success. When he is promoted to the position of a President of a nation or company, you become the First lady of the nation or company and enjoy all the privileges attached to the office of the First Lady. If he becomes the Ambassador to a nation, you get to ride in the same car with him, not a lesser one. Husbands are crowns on the heads of

WOMAN – Created to Help

their wives and cause God's beauty upon their wives to be complete. In fact, it is the woman that showcases the financial success of her husband. You can tell about a man's financial success by the changes you see in his wife's choice of wardrobe and the way she walks. Her association begins to change as she begins to meet high profile personalities associated with her husband's position, and the way she talks changes too. Even the skin glows brighter. You notice that her fragrance changes and lingers on.

God's Beauty and great wealth shall be our portion in Jesus name.

Seek God's face on behalf of your husband. Be the praying wife who desires the good of your husband. If your husband comes home from his office with any challenge and informs you about it, do not just nod your head and allow it to rest like that. Go to God in prayer on his behalf. Hold his hands and pray together. Wake up in the middle of the night and seek God's face on the matter, supporting it with fasting if need be.

WOMAN – Created to Help

Let your husband know that his wife is always there praying for him. God is not a user of men, He blesses. He is a rewarder. There is nothing that a wife does to improve the life of her husband and her God-given children that goes in vain. There is always a pay day or rather, pay days from God.

Hebrews 11:6

6 But without faith it is impossible to please him: for he that cometh to God must believe that he is, and that he is a rewarder of them that diligently seek him.

7) Be a helper, not a destroyer of destiny

As a helper, the destiny of your family is in your hands. You are to make their lives better by partnering with God in prayer and doing what needs to be done as a Godly wife and mother. Some women have destroyed what was committed into their hands through idleness and an "I don't care" attitude. The

WOMAN – Created to Help

Bible says that it is possible for a house to drop through by idleness.

Ecclesiastes 10:18

18 By much slothfulness the building decayeth; and through idleness of the hands the house droppeth through.

When the blessing of God in your home becomes the reason for not praying as before or not going to church regularly, you need to be there to build up again in the place of prayer. Destinies are made on the altar of prayer. It is so easy to drift away from God when success comes, especially the man. The man gets so busy that he has little or no time for God or things that matter to God. You should be the helpmeet in such areas and pray him back. You are his wife for such a situation as this.

Be very relevant in your home so that you will not be displaced.

WOMAN – Created to Help

Some Key Areas to Be a Helper to Your Husband

1) Companionship

Be his helpmeet and companion as planned by God.

Genesis 2:18

18 And the Lord God said, It is not good that the man should be alone; I will make him an help meet for him.

Adam was lonely amidst all the animals and plants that God created in the garden of Eden. Nothing in the garden looked like him. He could not relate well with them even though he had authority over them.

The people around your husband in the workplace are not his companion. The friends out there cannot fill your space in his life. When a man feels better or satisfied hanging out with friends or colleagues rather than being with his family, there is danger. It means the house is on fire and at the edge of

WOMAN – Created to Help

breaking. There is nowhere more secured or comfortable than the home. Even if a home is as small as a rat hole, it is still home for the owner. That is his castle. If your presence is causing your husband and children to feel tensed, you need to seek God's face. The mother is always the anchor of a home that is filled with joy and laughter.

Be the solid rock that makes your home to stand and be the soft comforting pillow that your husband will rest on whenever he gets home after the day's work.

Most of the time when my husband is out of the country, I make sure that I see him on video calls. I remember once when I was watching him fall asleep during a video call. You may not be physically where your husband is, that does not mean you should not be part of him daily. Call him to find out how his day had been and pray together always. It is a common practice in my family to study the books of the Bible together as a family, even with my husband outside the country.

WOMAN – Created to Help

Distance should be no barrier. Technology has made the world a small village.

2) Sex

We are all sexual beings as created by God. It is for procreation and for bonding in the context of marriage.

Sex is so important to men that women as helpers must not take this lightly. Many homes have, unfortunately, been destroyed by sex-related issues. We were created as women to help our husbands in this area. Sex cannot be delegated. Have you ever seen a woman who loves her friend so much that she asks her to help keep her husband warm on the bed while she goes on official assignment? That role is meant for you and for you alone.

WOMAN – Created to Help

A woman must be ready to satisfy her husband sexually. Never use it as a weapon of revenge or for money. Be available for your man always.

1 Corinthians 7:2-5

2 Nevertheless, to avoid fornication, let every man have his own

wife, and let every woman have her own husband.

3 Let the husband render unto the wife due benevolence: and likewise also the wife unto the husband.

4 The wife hath not power of her own body, but the husband: and likewise also the husband hath not power of his own body, but the wife.

5 Defraud ye not one the other, except it be with consent for a time, that ye may give yourselves to fasting and prayer; and come together again, that Satan tempt you not for your incontinency.

WOMAN – Created to Help

Do not starve your husband sexually by being too spiritual.

Proverbs 27:7

7 A satisfied soul loathes the honeycomb,

But to a hungry soul every bitter thing is sweet.

Sex outside marriage is bitter. We should not allow bitterness to come into our homes by denying our husband sex. You are made to help him fulfil his God-ordained assignment.

Be creative in your sex life. Try different styles and have it everywhere in your home. Toilet, bathroom, and even on the floor of your kitchen when your kids are not around.

Make it a practice to shower together. It is a proven fact that couples who sleep together on the bed naked bond together better. It is skin to skin, no barrier.

Get a special night gown for special nights in your bedroom. Pastor Mrs. Funke Felix Adejumo calls it transparent honesty.

WOMAN – Created to Help

Don't go to bed with the same night wear that you used while preparing stew in the kitchen and is now smelling of the stew.

Wash up, perfume your body and be ready for him.

Take yourselves out for dinner. No child is allowed on such outings, just you and your husband. Check in to hotels sometimes for a change of environment - just two of you. Life is sweet and marriage is very sweet when in God's plan.

If you ensure that your husband is filled up, no strange woman will be able to seduce him.

Be your husband's mistress and wife at the same time. Have you ever wondered why some men go to mistresses? The conduct of a man who was welcomed home in hot weather with creamy ice cream or cold water in a clean glass cup would be different from that of a man who was welcomed home with nothing but nagging and complaints. Where do you think a man would rather be? Your guess is as good as mine.

WOMAN – Created to Help

Remember, HIV/AIDS is the gift from harlots. That shall not be our portion in Jesus' name.

Let me tell you one small secret. The more you are available to satisfy your husband sexually, the more the cheques will continue to roll in and the more he will be willing to entrust you with his Card PIN number. Think about it. A happy husband leads to more cash transfer.

I will tell you another secret that can get you and your husband powerfully connected to God. Sex time can be used as a time of agreement to seek God's face. The Bible says he who goes to the harlot, takes up the spirit of the harlot.

1 Corinthians 6:16

16 What? know ye not that he which is joined to an harlot is one body? for two, saith he, shall be one flesh.

Sex connects you spiritually with your wife and you can both pray more effectively with one spirit and one voice.

WOMAN – Created to Help

19 Again I say unto you, That if two of you shall agree on earth as touching any thing that they shall ask, it shall be done for them of my Father which is in heaven.

3) Food

There is a popular saying that, the way to a man's heart is through his stomach. As women, we should be there to give our husbands good and healthy food that will take them away from unnecessary visits to the fast food joints. We should be ready to prepare the venison that will make their hearts to be filled with joy and satisfaction which in turn leads to an outpouring of blessings from them to us. The prayer of a husband for his wife works like magic. When I first started to search for a job in the UK, I put in all that I could, but I had no job offer. One morning as my husband was preparing for

WOMAN – Created to Help

work, I knelt before him and asked him to pray for me. That same week, I got a job. See, a husband's sincere blessing works.

Genesis 25:21

21 And Isaac intreated the Lord for his wife, because she was barren: and the Lord was intreated of him, and Rebekah his wife conceived.

Men love their food. Be ready to do your part. Some men want fresh food every day. They would have no stale food or leftovers from the fridge. This is a bit tough sometimes, but with God all things are possible. If you do not help in this area, your husband may go out to satisfy himself with the Delilahs that are waiting for him.

Proverbs 7:10-18

10 And, behold, there met him a woman with the attire of an harlot, and subtil of heart.

WOMAN – Created to Help

11 (She is loud and stubborn; her feet abide not in her house:

12 Now is she without, now in the streets, and lieth in wait at every corner.)

13 So she caught him, and kissed him, and with an impudent face said unto him,

14 I have peace offerings with me; this day have I payed my vows.

15 Therefore came I forth to meet thee, diligently to seek thy face, and I have found thee.

16 I have decked my bed with coverings of tapestry, with carved works, with fine linen of Egypt.

17 I have perfumed my bed with myrrh, aloes, and cinnamon.

18 Come, let us take our fill of love until the morning: let us solace ourselves with loves.

WOMAN – Created to Help

The internet has made life so easy. Go to YouTube and upgrade yourself in this area. Learning has no age limit. If you stop learning you will start dying.

I had to go on YouTube to learn new things when I went to the Middle East to see my husband, so that my marriage could be upgraded in that area. I knew the snacks that my husband enjoys most. I made sure I gave these to him always, especially on weekends.

Please do not just keep yourself busy on Facebook without getting anything useful for your home. Don't just look at other people's pictures or the latest designer clothes.

Be the 21st century woman.

4) Outward Appearance

Looking good they say is good business. Make it your business to look good for your husband.

WOMAN – Created to Help

Males are designed by God to be attracted to beautiful things while women are moved by what they hear. Tell a woman that she is beautiful, and you would have made her day. She would go around bubbling with joy and stay close to the mirror all day, smiling.

Men are turned on by the beautiful appearances presented to them by their wives. What view is your husband seeing?

Some people spend so much to buy houses with a good view. For the man, a view is not enough, it must be an attractive one. For some, it is the green grass or trees that count and for others, it is the blue sea. Whatever view appeals to your husband, make sure it is available for him to keep him at home. Make your appearance a good view worth staying or coming home for.

Many men or husbands have been driven away from homes because of unattractive views. They come home late because the view at home is not interesting.

WOMAN – Created to Help

Did you notice Adam's reaction when he saw Eve? He screamed, this is bone of my bone and flesh of my flesh! Why? Because of the view that he saw. Men pursue beauty. They tend towards beautiful things.

Genesis 2:23

23 And Adam said, This is now bone of my bones, and flesh of

my flesh: she shall be called Woman, because she was taken out of Man.

Remember your husband goes out daily and works with women who may be more beautiful than you. And perhaps they know how to put colours together and look beautiful.

Your dressing does not have to be expensive if you cannot afford expensive things now. Life is in phases and men are in sizes. Live your size per time.

WOMAN – Created to Help

There are so many ways you can look your best and not break the bank. It is not all designer stores that are expensive if you know your way around. Sales time is always the best time to buy. The African wax cloth, for instance, is not very expensive. There are beautiful designs that are cheap, and you will still look elegant in them.

Thrift stores are there if you know how to make your picks. Start small and end big.

I encourage you to look good always. Take care of your hair and perfume your body. Body and mouth odour can drive our husbands away from us. Brush your teeth before going to bed. Get used to mouth wash and floss your teeth if you can. Good breath is an asset.

Be tidy physically. If a woman has long hair, it is considered as a glory and covering. That's what the Bible says.

1 Corinthians 11:15

WOMAN – Created to Help

Always carry tidy hair. Make your hair regularly. Avoid wearing the same hair for too long, it smells and disrupts bedroom intimacy. Part of the first thing that attracts a woman to men is the hair. You hear some men commenting on your hair if it looks beautiful. That is where the glory is. If you are a wig person, make sure it is clean. Maintain it well. You do not have to break the bank because of human hair. Cut your coat according to your cloth, not according to your size. If your size is too big for the cloth, just turn the cloth into a beautiful head or neck scarf and you will still look beautiful.

Sometimes we take our husbands for granted. We think that because we are married, nothing more needs to be done to make us look attractive. We stop doing all the things we were doing that made us look like wife material for our husbands. We now start looking like his grandma, just because we do not

"

care anymore. One thing every woman should remember is that, this man is human and is moved by what he sees. If he sees a good-looking secretary at work all day long and then an untidy grandma-looking wife at home, hmm, there is a potential problem. Let us flee all appearances of evil.

Make your husband so proud of your look that he will always be eager to introduce you to his friends and colleagues. Be the attractive woman.

Most of the time, we are the architects of what happens in our homes, it is not always the enemy that is to blame.

5) Home and financial management

Dirty and untidy homes can be a source of divorce or stress in a home. Women, let us live clean. Make your home desirable for your husband. It is not only when visitors are coming that we should start thinking of tidying up our homes. Cleanliness

WOMAN – Created to Help

is next to Godliness; the common saying goes. God could not visit the children of Israel until they washed their clothes. He told Moses to instruct them to wash their clothes and be ready for His visitation.

Exodus 19:10

10 And the Lord said unto Moses, Go unto the people, and sanctify them today and to morrow, and let them wash their clothes,

Let your house be clutter-free. Do not buy or gather items that you don't need just because there are sales at the shops. You will end up filling your house with junks. Allow fresh air to flow freely in your home for good health.

Some people have a habit of leaving dirty plates in the bedroom and causing the room to have an unpleasant odour. This could make a man stay out of his home. Use the air freshener when it becomes necessary but good hygiene is crucial. Open your windows for fresh air. There is tendency for the house and clothes to smell stale when your doors and windows are shut all the time. Clean the house regularly and do not allow your home to become a breeding ground for rodents.

Sometimes, we think we can leave our bedroom anyhow because no visitor comes in there. We should realise that a good bedroom is an invitation for romance in marriage. When your bedroom is clean and the bed is well laid with clean bed sheets of pleasant colour and design, your husband will be comfortable staying in the bedroom and be ready to welcome his wife for the night.

Did you hear what the harlot in Proverbs 7:16-17 says?

Proverbs 7:16-17

16 I have decked my bed with coverings of tapestry, with carved works, with fine linen of Egypt.

WOMAN – Created to Help

Change your bed sheets regularly, especially if you live in a place where the weather is hot, and you have a lot of dust settling around the room. Make sure your towels are in good shape. Do not wait for your white towels to turn brown before you change them. If you cannot maintain white colour, go for brown or green, but make sure you wash your towels regularly. Remember that your bed is not a storage place for your undies. Put things in their proper places. Do your laundering regularly and ensure your clothes are well ironed. It baffles me when I see some men in rough shirts or trousers. The first question that comes to my mind is, where was his wife when he left home? Why should you allow your husband to leave home without checking to make sure that he is a good representative of the Most High God in appearance? Remember that he is a Royal Priesthood.

WOMAN – Created to Help

Leave no room for the strange woman to take your place. Men are moved by what they see. Being married to a good man is not a ticket for shabbiness and sluggishness. Be up and doing to make your home attractive to your husband.

People have been known to receive revelations from God even on their toilet seats. Some people read their Bibles while sitting on it. Imagine a toilet seat that is dirty and smelling. Will you or your husband be able to sit comfortably on it and receive what God has to say?

I learn everyday because I am work in progress.

Do we want God's presence in our homes always? Let us tidy up. Where the presence of God is, there is fullness of joy.

Psalm 16:11

11 Thou wilt shew me the path of life: in thy presence is fulness of joy; at thy right hand there are pleasures for evermore.

WOMAN – Created to Help

Money management is one key area where a woman should remain relevant on the home front. Some women have proved themselves so trustworthy in financial management that their husbands can readily entrust them with their bank card PIN but there are others who are not there yet. They are still work in progress. The moment some women know how much their husband has; it is party time. That is the time to clean out the old clothes from the wardrobe and replace them with new ones. It is time to buy gold and diamond. The vacation that has been long due suddenly becomes an urgent matter and the family must now go on that expensive vacation.

No future plan in view. You must have a plan for your future. Someone says not to wear the cement for your future house as a gold necklace today. There is time for everything. The clothes that you bought today will be of no value tomorrow. But the house you build today will always be valuable any time. Clothes can go out of fashion but houses rarely go out of use if they are well constructed. I have heard about centuries old buildings that still sell for millions of pounds in the United Kingdom.

Help your husband to invest in his future. Time waits for no one.

Men are very sensitive to things like this. Be the helper of your husband's financial destiny. You were created to be in his life for such an assignment.

6) Respect

Respect means to hold someone in high regard or to praise and to speak highly of him. Of all the things that I have talked about, the most important is respect. If a man is not getting the other items I mentioned, he can get them outside. Nothing hurts a man like disrespect from his wife. It makes a man to feel as little as breadcrumbs.

WOMAN – Created to Help

Negative words spoken to men stick to them like magnet to metal. They are like sharp arrows piercing their hearts and they do not forget easily. It is easier for a woman to get out of emotional trauma than a man. If a man is unfaithful in marriage, the woman can easily forgive him especially after an apology from the man or intervention by highly respected elders or pastors. She may not totally forget, but she can forgive the man. If it is the woman who is unfaithful, the man does not forgive so easily.

Even if a man is without a cent or penny to his name, the moment you agreed to be his wife, he deserves your respect and you must give him your respect always. Nothing destroys homes like lack of respect for the head of the family.

Philippians 2:3

3 Let nothing be done through strife or vainglory; but in lowliness of mind let each esteem other better than themselves.

WOMAN – Created to Help

Do not give honour or respect to your pastor and disrespect your husband. This is not good. Dr Myles Monroe said in one of his teachings that he sent a woman who was his church member home from a prayer meeting because the husband was home and she was in church at the time that was supposed to be dinner time for the family. The woman's husband was so shocked that a pastor could send his wife home to come and take care of the family. This made the man to join his wife in that church. Pastors must encourage women to respect their husbands according to the word of God. Do not make church activities to become more important than the husband that your church member left at home. Families are going through tough times in their relationships which God had originally designed to be perfect and full of His love.

Some women start respecting their husbands when the bank account starts to look good. This is not good at all. Be your husband's number one cheer leader. Whether there is money

WOMAN – Created to Help

in the bank or not does not matter. What matters is your unity and trust in God. Unity and love in the home attracts Godly wealth. You know why? Your prayers are answered speedily when you love each other and pray with one vision and one voice. The word of God says, if two of you shall agree as touching a thing…

Matthew 18:19

19 Again I say unto you, That if two of you shall agree on earth as touching any thing that they shall ask, it shall be done for them of my Father which is in heaven.

Speak kindly to him even when you are angry. Never insult him in the presence of his children, friends and family members. Do all your arguments behind closed doors and be the best of friends outside even if you are angry.

If you sell your husband cheap, nobody will put a great price on him. Be all over him in the public. Serve his food at parties

WOMAN – Created to Help

if allowed. Give him the best portion of meat from your pot. Do not give him the part that you do not like. There is great blessing in this.

Never ague in the presence of your children. It removes respect from their dad, and from you as well. And what example are you giving the children? Think about your grandchildren's generation. Whatever foundation you lay for your children now is what they will pass on to their own families.

Women, let us be the helpers that we were created to be.

The 360 Degree woman is exceptional in all areas. She is loving, caring and honourable to her family. Love your husband with all your heart. Lust after him and show it to him to the point that other men planning to get married will be praying for a woman like you in their lives.

WOMAN – Created to Help

Be his number one cheer leader. Respect him publicly. Men are respect conscious. Someone said that if a man has the money, he can decide to eat out in the best restaurant, if his wife fails to give him good food at home; he can decide to sleep with other women if his wife denies him sex at home, though with the gift of HIV/AIDS.

Without any doubt, respect is number one for the man. I recently listened to a tape by Pastor Bimbo Odukoya where she talked about respect for husbands. She said a woman in her church normally called her husband by name. The woman went to her husband's office to say hello and while there, the husband's secretary asked if the man wanted tea and to every question the man asked her, she responded with a very respectful 'yes sir'. This wife was so surprised that she made up her mind to change her attitude towards her husband. When her husband got home that day, she attended to him with the words "yes sir", The man was surprised and asked her what

WOMAN – Created to Help

had changed? She simply responded to her husband that this was the new her.

A very wise woman. She did not waste time at all.

Please, woman, if there is something lacking in your marriage and you are privileged to know the right thing, please change before it is too late. Get knowledge and wisdom. Learn from other people's mistakes. Develop yourself both in appearance and intellectually. Do not be a 14th century wife in the 21st century. You will be left behind. Do not allow your seat to be vacant. There are many Delilahs out there.

When I went to the Middle East to spend some time with my husband, God opened my eyes to a few things and taught me some new skills. You never stop learning in your marriage and there is no end to learning as a woman or wife.

Thursday is the beginning of the weekend in the Middle East so, I would go on YouTube to learn something new to prepare

WOMAN – Created to Help

for my husband as a special weekend meal. I would bake fresh bread, roast chicken, make different snacks and Scotch eggs just for him to enjoy the weekend. I was always preparing new dishes and snacks to make him remember me after I travelled back to Canada.

What will your husband remember you for?

What will make him run home from work, singing at the end of the working day?

Some men pick up all the overtime to stay away from home to have some peace. This does not bode well for the family. As women, we are the ones who determine the aroma of the home.

We determine what the temperature is at home.

Let us be that Helper that God has created us to be.

Our attitude to our husbands will determine their success and invariably our own success too.

WOMAN – Created to Help

We were created to help them achieve God's purpose in their lives and as we do, our own purpose will be achieved gloriously.

Naturally, I am not an early riser because I sleep very late, sometimes I sleep around 2am. But I had to wake up early to prepare breakfast for my husband and pack his lunch before he went to work. It felt a bit uncomfortable at first, but I quickly turned to my Helper, God the Father to ask for grace and strength. I prayed to God to make me enjoy cooking for my husband so early and as I did, I also asked God to give me my own thing. God heard my heartfelt prayer and gave me the inspiration for the book "What is in your Pillow?". Love your husband as God commanded and see God bless you in return.

We do not have to struggle for money as women. All we need do is to pray for our husbands to succeed and ask for divine ideas for us too to be financially free and be supportive to our husbands.

WOMAN – Created to Help

You are an asset, not a liability.

When the Helper is Not on Duty as Required

I have a word here for those who think the helper is not important in homes. When a woman ceases to be fully committed to her marriage, and does whatever seems right to her, or she is not allowed by cultural practices to do what she is meant to be doing in her home, the progress or upward movement of the family starts to experience deterioration. Affection becomes aggression. Love turns to hatred and compassion turns to depression. The family ties become so weak that a small ant can break them.

Lack of commitment to your marriage as a team member breeds disobedient children like the children of Samuel.

1 Samuel 8:3-5.

3 And his sons walked not in his ways, but turned aside after lucre, and took bribes, and perverted judgment.

WOMAN – Created to Help

4 Then all the elders of Israel gathered themselves together, and came to Samuel unto Ramah,

5 And said unto him, Behold, thou art old, and thy sons walk not in thy ways: now make us a king to judge us like all the nations.

The question to ask is, "where was their mother?" We should understand that Samuel's assignment was a time consuming one and his wife should have been there to take care of the home. Sometimes we exempt our children from discipline at a certain age. We overlook most of the things they are doing wrong. If our focus is to make our children responsible and to showcase the beauty of God in their lives, then, there should be no time when we cannot correct them in love. Remember that our children may bring pain to us and to themselves in the future if we don't discipline them now. We as parents, especially the women, are answerable to God.

Our spouses too become lukewarm and discouraged when we are not at our duty post. The once peaceful, closely knitted family

WOMAN – Created to Help

becomes a family of islands, each island for one person. I for myself and you for yourself. No care, no love.

Each person starts to look outside for love. Looking for approval where indeed there is none. There can be no vacuum in life. In family life, parents must be there for their children to fill up the vacuum with tender love and care.

No one can love you more than yourself and your immediate family.

In so many homes, the woman abandons her duty post and allows her husband to single-handedly run the home while she is busy acquiring dollars in a bid to compete with the husband financially.

A day is coming when all our possessions will become nothing. The care, love and discipline we instilled in our children are the things that will be remembered. Our parenting duties will be put to test. One day, we will give account of all the things that we failed to do in the lives of our husbands and children.

WOMAN – Created to Help

Parenting is like making down payments for our future homes. If we do not invest positively now in our family or homes, there will be no harvest in the future.

The highly admired Proverbs 31 woman is free financially but maintains a good balance in her family life. She is a Godly and a great wife and is liberal in her giving.

Some women, instead of feeding their household with good food, leave their house helps to take care of the children and cook for their husbands. And then we wonder why some men are leaving their wives for strange women or even sleeping with the house helps.

Total or partial neglect of our duties as women is degrading the perfect family which God designed in the garden of Eden. Violence is taking over our homes. Parents are pitched against each other and children have discarded family values. No more family time. Family altars and family dinner times have gone missing in many homes.

WOMAN – Created to Help

Technologies have taken over and the love of money has replaced people's love for their families.

Woman, wake up and take your place in destiny. God is watching what you are doing with the responsibilities that He placed in your hands.

Nothing must die in your hands.

Chapter 4 – A WORD OF ENCOURAGEMENT

Every Woman is Unique

A woman is uniquely made for her unique assignment. There is no conflict in our assignments. Women should be free to pursue their God-ordained purpose. There should be no strife or envy. You do your own and I do mine to make the world a better place for all of us. Elizabeth the mother of John the Baptist was never envious of Mary the mother of Jesus even though she was older than Mary. She knew her place in destiny and gave honour to the carrier of the Saviour of the world. She understood who she was carrying and the Gift that Mary was carrying. One child was to prepare the way and the other child was to die for humanity to be reconciled back to God.

Two clear assignments!

WOMAN – Created to Help

Woman, whether you are single and waiting for the man that God has sent you to help, or you are married and waiting for the fruit of the womb, let God meet you serving in His vineyard. Do something for God while waiting. Do not be idle, do not pull down other people's homes or destinies. Wait patiently.

Psalms 40:1-3

I waited patiently for the Lord; and he inclined unto me, and heard my cry.

2 He brought me up also out of an horrible pit, out of the miry clay, and set my feet upon a rock, and established my goings.

3 And he hath put a new song in my mouth, even praise unto our God: many shall see it, and fear, and shall trust in the Lord.

Eve was made for Adam. For every man, there is an Eve made by God. Not every woman is yours as a man. Also, not every man is yours as a woman. Not every dress is custom made for you. David

WOMAN – Created to Help

was given king Saul's war garment to fight Goliath but could not achieve God's purpose until he got his own weapon – the 5 stones.

Do not put on another woman's husband, he does not have your name attached to his. Doing that can only bring frustration and destruction of destinies. It is like wrong blood transfusion. It brings instant death.

A Word for Singles

For singles who are in line for marriage, I believe God is preparing you for that man that is meant for you. God wants you to be suitable for the man. Let your purpose in life be from God; not from man or from the internet. The internet has so many solutions to whatever problem you can think of. The question is, Are all those solutions Godly? If your life is totally dependent on information from the internet, I am not sure what your life will look like. I am not saying that you should not look for information on the internet, especially messages from anointed servants of God,

WOMAN – Created to Help

all I am saying is that, your first point of call should be God who knows all things and has the answer to all life situations. Look unto God for the provision of the man that your heart desires. It is quite possible for God to direct you to the internet for an answer but check with Him first.

Psalm 34:5

5 They looked unto him, and were lightened: and their faces were not ashamed.

God provides illumination to any dark situation that you may be in. He wants us to depend on Him totally, both in small and in big situations.

Jeremiah 17:5

5 Thus saith the Lord; Cursed be the man that trusteth in man, and maketh flesh his arm, and whose heart departeth from the Lord.

Remember that God said, "I will make him a helpmeet". Which means, God is the one who can make you to be the help that is

WOMAN – Created to Help

meet (suitable) for the man. You cannot make yourself, neither can you give yourself to any man.

 Release yourself for God to make you suitable for that God-ordained man. If you want to make yourself, you will look for the man yourself. How far can your eyes see? Can you see as far as God would see? Even if you can see, do you know the intent of that man's heart? A man, may be good outside but be terrible on the inside

To you, that man might tick all your boxes about your heart's desires, he may be tall, rich, handsome but what about the inner man?

You need the help of God to see the inside of a man. Outward look or material possessions are not all that matter. Remember the heart of man is desperately wicked.

Jeremiah 17:9

WOMAN – Created to Help

Be submissive to God's instructions. Practice submissiveness with God and it will be so easy to submit to the man in your life.

I watched a video clip on the 700 Club, a Christian TV broadcast show. It was about a woman who was suddenly divorced without her prior knowledge. She said there was no argument before she left home; her husband suddenly announced to her that he was divorcing her. Guess what God told this woman? God told her to love the husband more.

What? That's not the answer anyone would expect but that is God for you. His ways are totally different from ours.

She was submissive to God's instructions and at the end won back her husband and the second honeymoon started.

Single ladies, never allow anyone to rush you into what is not in God's plan for you. To God, age is nothing. He created time that

WOMAN – **Created to Help**

makes up your age. God is not held back by time. Being advanced in age does not mean you should take a step that will lead to lifelong regret. Because your mates or sisters are married has nothing to do with the time set for you by God. Nobody will be there with you. You will bear the pain alone. Be careful, stay focused and trust God. No woman is created to be alone. None shall lack her mate, the Bible says.

Isaiah 34:16

16 Seek ye out of the book of the Lord, and read: no one of these shall fail, none shall want her mate: for my mouth it hath commanded, and his spirit it hath gathered them.

The journey of marriage is life long. The door of marriage has one handle and the handle is outside which makes the door to be opened easily. At the back, there is no handle. Coming out is difficult and painful. Divorce is not as easy as one may think. It takes something out of someone's life. Part of you will be gone

WOMAN – Created to Help

with the man. And it brings violence to the fabric of marriage. God hates divorce.

Malachi 2:16

16 For the Lord, the God of Israel, saith that he hateth putting away: for one covereth violence with his garment, saith the Lord of hosts: therefore take heed to your spirit, that ye deal not treacherously.

That is why you must be so sure of who you want to spend the rest of your life with. You need God all the way.

Parents, please do not take the place of God in your children's lives. Allow God to make them and to choose for them. Do not push them out in a hurry because your friend's children are getting married and yours have not. God has a set time for everyone's marital destiny. Do not think that a man is good for your daughter when you have not consulted God who gave you the daughter to care for on His behalf.

WOMAN – Created to Help

The making and building of a woman in preparation for the assignment from God is very profitable.

A Word for Single Parents

In case there is no man in your life, and you are a parent, I would like to say that your relevance is not affected at all. God brought a complete woman to help Adam in every situation that was unsatisfactory in his life. There will always be someone like an Adam around every woman. It could be your son, daughter, colleague or friends that you are destined to help.

Perhaps you have been wronged by your former husband. If you had children for him, please do not sow the seed of bitterness in them. You never know what God has in stock for you. This man may come back by the divine intervention of God. We have seen so many testimonies of such. Hold your head up with your shoulders straight and do what God wants you to do per time. If you prevent your children from seeing their father, when they grow

WOMAN – Created to Help

up and become free from your guidance, they will look for their dad and forgive him. Who does not need a father? In case the father is ready to be part of the children's lives financially especially in their education, my advice would be that you should let him take up his responsibilities in that area. No matter how wealthy you are, let him do it. Do not overwhelm yourself with unnecessary burdens. You can do any other thing that needs to be done for the children. Save your money for your future. You will need it. You do not want to depend on your children for financial support in old age. It feels good to be self sufficient financially in old age. The Bible says a good man leaves inheritance for his children's children. It applies to both man and woman. This is my own understanding.

Proverbs 13:22

A good man leaveth an inheritance to his children's children: and the wealth of the sinner is laid up for the just.

WOMAN – Created to Help

In case it was a woman who brought you pain in your marriage, do not embark on revenge rampage by going after another woman's husband. The battle is not yours, leave it for God.

Romans 12:19

19 Dearly beloved, avenge not yourselves, but rather give place unto wrath: for it is written, Vengeance is mine; I will repay, saith the Lord.

Women are created to build homes with God and to raise Godly seed that will build God's Kingdom. There is always something good in marriage. If we place ourselves in the mighty Hands of God to help us, the word divorce will be very scarce in our midst, especially in the body of Christ.

There is no perfect man or woman anywhere; everyone is working towards perfection. The issue is, we are looking to fill the 20% deficiencies in our spouses forgetting the 80% good qualities that are already in them. We keep chasing a moving target and soon

WOMAN – Created to Help

become frustrated and the next thing we are thinking about is divorce.

God hates divorce. It is the root of violence in our society and in the whole world.

The truth is that not every woman is truly occupying the divine position that God has assigned to her. A lot of us are not helping our husbands at all. A helper must be ready to face the challenges involved in helping others. To be effective on the job, we must understand that storms will come, and we will face discouragement along the way. That is why every woman must be knowledgeable about what it takes to be the help that is meet for her husband. There is no substitute for knowledge. Go after it and at all cost. As I said in an earlier chapter, the time has come for every woman to be fully engaged in the unique assignment given to her by God.

In the book of Revelation chapter two, Jesus was addressing each of the seven churches in Asia minor according to His expectations from them. No church was treated the same way. Jesus introduced

WOMAN – Created to Help

Himself to each church in a unique way, highlighting who He was to them and what made them different from the others. To the church in Smyrna, He was the First and the Last, the One who was dead and is alive. To the church of Ephesus, He was the One with the seven stars in His right hand, who walks amid the seven golden candlesticks. To the church in Pergamos, He was the One with the sharp swords with two edges.

One common phrase that Jesus said to all the churches is "I Know Your Works".

What does this mean? It means that our callings are different, and God is going to ask us questions about the assignment He gave to us. There is no need for us as women to compete; we are to work together in unity and love, helping one another to get to that glorious destiny that God has prepared for us.

Remember what I said, that no woman was made just to occupy empty space; you were CREATED TO HELP.

WOMAN – Created to Help

For once, women, let us discover who we really are and why we were created.

Let us stay at our duty posts minding our God-assigned duty. Enough of walking in someone else's path, creating chaos and frustrating destinies.

Joel 2:8

8 Neither shall one thrust another; they shall walk every one in his path: and when they fall upon the sword, they shall not be wounded.

From henceforth, there shall be no more confusion about who we are as women in Jesus name.

No strange woman will take your place in your husband's life in Jesus name.

WOMAN – Created to Help

A Word for Widows

God's plan for his children is to live long and have a fulfilled life. Some things happen that are out of our control like the death of loved ones. In such difficult situations, the only hope is in God. He said he will be the husband of the widow and father to the fatherless. He even instructed the children of Israel to treat the widows and the fatherless well. Widows and the fatherless are very close to the heart of God. They are special to Him.

Deuteronomy 24:17

17 Thou shalt not pervert the judgment of the stranger, nor of the fatherless; nor take a widow's raiment to pledge:

Deuteronomy 24:21

21 When thou gatherest the grapes of thy vineyard, thou shalt not glean it afterward: it shall be for the stranger, for the fatherless, and for the widow.

WOMAN – Created to Help

In this situation, you should hold firm your faith and trust in God. You should commit your life and those of your children into God's hand, asking Him to be what your husband could not be to you and your children.

If you desire to be married again, you should seek God's face for divine direction. I believe God will choose for you if you put your trust in God. If you do not want to remarry, you are still very relevant in life. Your children are there to be nurtured, if you are blessed with children. If not, there will be other people around you whom God has elevated you to nurture. Your relevance in life is still very intact.

A Word for Someone Special

A quick word to that special person reading this book, especially if you are woman who thinks you have been left alone with so much on your shoulder. You may be a single woman trusting God for a Godly husband and it looks as if nothing is happening. Maybe no

WOMAN – Created to Help

man is looking at you or you have gone through many disappointed relationships. One thing is certain, the word of God is yea and Amen. God is Truth and there is no untruth in Him. He said that He will not leave you nor forsake you. He will surely bring His word to pass.

Deuteronomy 31:6

6 Be strong and of a good courage, fear not, nor be afraid of them: for the Lord thy God, he it is that doth go with thee; he will not fail thee, nor forsake thee.

Or maybe you feel you have not been able to help that man. The strength that you need is in God. Why not surrender your strength to God and allow Him to help you? Remember He made you and made you for a purpose. All you need do is go to Him. He is waiting with open hands. Have your rest in Him. He is in total control.

Matthew 11:28

WOMAN – Created to Help

28 Come unto me, all ye that labour and are heavy laden, and I will give you rest.

Any journey in the wrong direction can start all over again and you can trust God for divine speed.

Nothing is too late to change.

It is not over until you say it with your mouth.

Romans 10:10

10 For with the heart man believeth unto righteousness; and with the mouth confession is made unto salvation.

You were created to Help.

You can boldly confess that,

I AM CREATED TO BE A HELPER AND THAT WILL I BE IN JESUS NAME.

WOMAN – Created to Help

A Word for Men

It was because of the Father's love for the man that He created the woman to make his life beautiful and full of God's glory.

As much as your wife is expected to help you in fulfilling your assignment; it rests on you, the man, to make your wife's role in your life an easy one. Give her all the information she needs to complete her tasks accurately and on time. Incomplete information or a lack of it may hinder her from accomplishing her task as a God-sent helper. Companies make out time to orientate or train their new employees for the job. They share important information about the organization, its work groups, its processes and its expectations. At the end of the training or orientation, the new employees know enough to get them started on the job.

In the same way, a husband, as the head of the family, should know his vision and be prepared to share it with his wife.

Clear and sincere communication of vision is important for success in marriage. Your helper needs this.

WOMAN – Created to Help

Adam might have told Eve about the danger of eating the forbidden fruit in the garden of Eden. I believe the reason they fell to the deception of Satan was because they did not fully understand their identity in God. Satan told Eve that eating the fruit would not lead to death but would make them as wise as God. Maybe Eve was told by Adam that they were created in the image and likeness of God and had the same capacity to operate like their heaven Father, forgetting that like begets like. A child of God is definitely a god. Being created in the image and likeness of God already conferred on them the capacity to operate like God.

Genesis 3:4-5

4 And the serpent said unto the woman, Ye shall not surely die:

5 For God doth know that in the day ye eat thereof, then your eyes shall be opened, and ye shall be as gods, knowing good and evil.

In today's workplace, Adam and Eve might have been sent to regular refresher courses to remind them about God's standing

WOMAN – Created to Help

instructions and to keep them in alignment with God's original plan for them.

Married couples should constantly engage in productive discussions and remind themselves about God's plan for the family.

We must not forget the fact that some men are naturally stubborn or difficult to work with. They know they need a God-sent helper, but the male ego would not allow them to accept the helper or the help. If men were designed to be self-sufficient, God would not have wasted His time to create women. You need your wife by your side, and not behind you as a subordinate or slave.

Any man who steps outside God's plan and calls his wife a bad name is directly saying, "I am the alpha and omega of my house and my family's new name is …."

If you call your wife 'Stupid', you will reap stupidity in your home because you automatically become 'Mr. and Mrs. Stupid' and your

WOMAN – Created to Help

children too will bear the same surname. We all know how important a name is in a person's destiny. Jabez was called sorrow and that was his life experience until he prayed to God for a change of name.

We reflect what we call ourselves. Do not call your wife a name that you are not ready to answer. It goes without saying that Mrs. Fool is married to Mr. Fool. When you hit your wife, you are hitting yourself. Remember she was created from your flesh and bone. And by the way, a man who goes on hitting himself needs medical attention. A word is enough for the wise.

Be a wise husband.

Love your wife unconditionally, the same way Christ loved you and He gave His life for you. Treat her as God has instructed you to.

Loving your wife means loving yourself. If you dislike her, other people would conclude that you chose the wrong helper or something ugly is happening to you. Seek God's face in your home.

Ephesians 5:25

25 Husbands, love your wives, even as Christ also loved the church, and gave himself for it;

Always remember that SHE WAS MADE FROM YOU AND SHE IS YOUR COMPANION.

Man, help your helper (your wife) to work with you in joy so that your own joy may be full.

How do you know that you need a helper?

Some assignments need some extra support from other people than the sent man to be fully achieved as God wants it. The saying that no man is an island is so true. No one was made to be successful all by himself. We all need God the giver of the assignment and what we call Helpers of destiny. These people are positioned to

WOMAN – Created to Help

make our assignments easier and positively effective. They make our journeys faster and interesting.

Every man or woman needs a helper at one point or another in life. It is not a question of "if you will need a helper", but "when you will need the helper". There are many indicators in life that tell us it is time to get a helper. Let's consider a few of these indicators.

1) Lack of speed or stagnation

When things come to a standstill or are not moving fast enough, you need a helper. When there is little or no progress in what you do, and when you are putting in all your effort, yet nothing seems to be happening.

The Bible says that two are better than one.

Ecclesiastes 4:9

9 Two are better than one,

Because they have a good reward for their labor.

WOMAN – Created to Help

One will chase a thousand and two will put ten thousand to flight. What a marvellous output. The effort of one man will take a longer time to show or to be effective. The Godly wisdom of the helper of destiny goes a long way in achieving our God ordained assignments.

2) The vision becomes bigger than the visionary

When God gives a man an assignment, it is always bigger than what he can do all by himself without the help of his wife. Many assignments or visions are supposed to be transgenerational. A great vision does not have to end with an individual. It must not die when the visionary dies. The beauty of success is in having a good successor. Success without a successor is failure.

Genesis 15:2-3

WOMAN – Created to Help

2 And Abram said, Lord God, what wilt thou give me, seeing I go childless, and the steward of my house is this Eliezer of Damascus?

3 And Abram said, Behold, to me thou hast given no seed: and, lo, one born in my house is mine heir.

Nobody wants his or her dream to end with them. It is always the desire of all to have someone who will carry on the assignment.

3) Lack of satisfaction

You are not likely to go far with anything you do if you do not derive joy or a sense of satisfaction from it. Just managing to get by can be very frustrating. We all know the frustration of working on a job where you are constantly looking forward to the next rest break or closing time. When you have lost your passion for your job or calling and are only working for the money, you need a helper. Your helper could be a counsellor or course tutor if you decide to re-train or take additional training.

4) The status quo is unsatisfactory

A feeling of total dissatisfaction with the situation at your current location could be an indication that you need a helper. An unsatisfactory situation could lead to unhappiness, frustration and loneliness. When God said, "It is not good that the man should be alone; I will make him an help meet for him", He must have seen through the mind of Adam. Rather than consign Adam to a lifetime of unhappiness, frustration and loneliness, God decided to do something quickly to make Adam fulfilled and satisfied. Perhaps, God thought of other solutions before deciding to create the woman. Creating the woman was God's best solution to Adam's unsatisfactory situation. All through the

WOMAN – Created to Help

ages, the woman has continued to be God's best solution to man's problems. You may think that my statement is biased because I am a woman. But we need to celebrate our women because they are specially created for special assignments. Thank You Lord.

Women are very special and dear to the heart of God. How do I know this?

Well, because God allowed the woman to be the carrier of The Messiah, Jesus Christ.

Woman, you were created because you were needed!!!

We need to know that every man or woman is on an assignment. That assignment is your purpose in life. To live a fulfilled life, everyone must find out what their purpose or assignment in life is.

Chapter 5 - LET US PRAY

Prayer of Faith

The identity problem cannot be solved with human wisdom. Accept Him as your personal Lord and Saviour today.

Do not delay as this may be too risky.

It is easier to give a good gift to the person who has a relationship with you than to a stranger. Except you belong to a family, you cannot enjoy the benefits the family enjoys

If you are not in a personal relationship with God, please do not let this moment pass you by. Embrace Him, He is closer to you than you think.

Please say this and mean it:

Dear Lord, I come to you today as a sinner

Please forgive me all my sins

WOMAN – Created to Help

I believe that Jesus is the son of God, He died on the cross to save me

On the third day He rose from the dead

Now I declare Him as my personal Lord and Saviour.

I ask You to wash me with the blood that was shed on Calvary's tree

From now I believe I am born again; I am a child of God.

Thank You Lord for saving me Amen.

Congratulations.

WOMAN – Created to Help

Personal Prayers

Married Women

Romans 8:11

11 But if the Spirit of him that raised up Jesus from the dead dwell in you, he that raised up Christ from the dead shall also quicken your mortal bodies by his Spirit that dwelleth in you.

As a helper assigned to a man, God has committed something great into your hands. God committed an only son into the hands of the Shunammite woman in 2 Kings 4. Her son became ill and was sent to her by his father, but this only child died.

1) I pray as a Helper of destiny that:

   a. Nothing committed into my hands by God shall die in Jesus name

   b. My children shall not die

   c. My marriage shall not die

WOMAN – Created to Help

    d. My husband shall fulfill his destiny

    e. No destinies connected to me shall die in Jesus name

2) I pray that the resurrection power of Jesus Christ will be at work:

    a. In my life

    b. In my home

    c. In my children

Anything that looks dead is resurrecting right now in Jesus name.

3) My womb, receive the life of Christ in Jesus' name.

4) I shall finish well and no strange woman shall take my place in my husband's life in Jesus name.

5) I shall not labour in vain.

Isaiah 62:8-9

WOMAN – Created to Help

8 The Lord has sworn by His right hand

And by the arm of His strength:

"Surely I will no longer give your grain

As food for your enemies;

And the sons of the foreigner shall not drink your new wine,

For which you have labored.

9 But those who have gathered it shall eat it,

And praise the Lord;

Those who have brought it together shall drink it in My holy

courts."

Singles

Psalm 68:6

WOMAN – Created to Help

6 God setteth the solitary in families: he bringeth out those which are bound with chains: but the rebellious dwell in a dry land.

1) God, make me visible to my God-ordained husband on time in Jesus name.

2) God, direct my steps to where my God ordained husband is in Jesus name.

3) God, build me and make me a suitable helper for my future husband.

Widows

Psalm 68:5

5 A father of the fatherless, and a judge of the widows, is God in his holy habitation.

1) God, place Your loving arms around me to help me in any situation I may be in right now in Jesus name.

WOMAN – Created to Help

2) God, place the aroma of Your love on me, fill the vacuum left by my husband and bless my children abundantly in Jesus name.

Divorcees

1) God, mend and restore my home in Jesus name.

Isaiah 58:12

And they that shall be of thee shall build the old waste places: thou shalt raise up the foundations of many generations; and thou shalt be called, The repairer of the breach, The restorer of paths to dwell in.

2) God, release my husband from the grip of the strange woman by the fire of the Holy Spirit, and bring him back home in Jesus name.

Proverbs 2:16

16 To deliver thee from the strange woman, even from the stranger which flattereth with her words;

WOMAN – Created to Help

WOMAN – Created to Help

Other Books by Titilayo Akinniyi

WOMAN – Created to Help